CW00409313

Text copyright © 2020 Caroline Gilpin

Front Cover Design – Kay Webb

Photo Image – Konstanttin/Shutterstock

FOR TIM

Who Believed In Me

Contents

PUTTING THE PIECES BACK TOGETHER

INTRODUCTION

This is not a self-help book. This is just a slice of my experience as a Christian who suffered a devastating loss. It's also a love story: a human love story and a divine love story. This is also unashamedly a Christian's response to loss.

Some people walk away when they feel God has deserted them: some of us cling on by our fingernails and, with God's grace, we will come out the other side. I am in the latter category: having barely clung on to the cliff face for a long time, I finally made my way back up on top and got back en-route with my journey with God.

When I lost my husband at a young age (he was forty-two and I was thirty-seven), I looked high and low for a Christian response to what I was going through: to find someone asking the same questions I was.

There are many good books out there on the stages of grieving or the minefields of going through loss. There are lots of excellent support groups out there and I found the secular group WAY (Widowed and Young) particularly helpful. The books and groups that I personally found helpful, I have listed at the back of this book.

However I found that very few books or groups addressed what happens when you believe God loves you yet lets you go through a tragedy. Was it all right to shout at God? Why had he abandoned me? Would I ever be able to trust him again? These were all questions for which I needed answers but couldn't find many people willing to talk about them and I didn't find a book written about them specifically relating to loss. I think this is the book I wish I had had at the time.

When I was baptised as an adult, aged twenty one, I was given a verse as a gift from my church: one which they believed that they had been directed to give me. It was Isaiah 43: 1 (RSV) – "Fear not for I have redeemed you; I have called you by name, you are mine." At the time, I thought it was lovely, inspiring and a verse I stuck on my wall to try to remember it but it didn't mean much other than that.

Years later, that verse has been a lifeline to me. It has become my bedrock from which I can't be moved. It has been God's promise to me on many occasions but particularly through my bereavement. The verses speak of God's love for me and his promise to get me through what he knew was coming. Verse one and the verses following have become really precious to me as they illustrate God's love story in my life:

"Fear not, for I have redeemed you; I have called you by name, you are my mine. (1b)

When you pass through the waters I will be with you; and through rivers, they shall not overwhelm you; when you walk through fire you shall not be burned, and the flame shall not consume you. (2)

For I am the LORD your God, the Holy One of Israel, your Saviour. I give Egypt as your ransom, Ethiopia and Seba in exchange for you. (3)

Because you are precious in my eyes and honoured, and I love you, I give men in return for you, peoples in exchange for your life." (4)

I was broken into pieces by my experience but I believe I have been re-shaped into something new. It's not necessarily better, it's definitely not something I would have chosen to be, life's just different from what I expected and so am I.

So if my experience can help you in any small way, please read on to find out about my love story, my small attempts at navigating through grief, mistakes I've made and lessons I've learned and through it all finding how to hang on to God's promise.

OUR LOVE STORY

I met my husband, Tim, in 1998. We were both what is politely called late bloomers! Both lacking in confidence in ourselves and our right to believe anyone would be interested in getting to know us, we were both in our thirties when we met, and had never had a serious relationship before. We had all but given up hope of it ever happening. Happily, we had mutual friends who introduced us. If you're expecting me to say we hit it off right away, sorry to disappoint you! I thought he was 'nice' but not my type. I know he liked me more than I liked him. He's not here to defend himself but he told me that much later!

Fortunately, we found some common subjects that we could both talk about for hours: a love of the night sky and space, Star Trek and the TV programme Northern Exposure, which was an obscure subject for most people at the time. My sister had video recordings of that said programme and something made me volunteer to lend him her collection...thanks to my sister for letting me!

So began an old fashioned postal correspondence with me sending a VHS tape and a note and Tim eventually responding when he'd had a chance to watch the episodes and wrote back for more. He was working shifts as a signalman in Cornwall at the time and I had no idea what shift work was like. It was totally alien territory to me but something I was to get to know well. He had a lifelong passion for all things related to the railway and, when he was made redundant, he decided to retrain and got the job of his dreams as a signalman in the Hereford area. Railways had

4

only been of passing interest to me: something I used occasionally to get to London from my home in Kent, or a holiday treat when I visited a preserve line to indulge in the nostalgia of steam. His passion was to become an integral part of our lives together and part of what I loved so much about him.

It's funny what you remember or think of years later: as a teen when my friends wrote lists of the perfect man for each of us, my list always included hands with long fingers like a musician. Tim's hands did not have long fingers but they became one of the features of him I loved most. They were hands that were calloused with work from pulling levers at the signal box and full of strength, yet so gentle – just like him.

I was living in Kent, he was living in Cornwall when we began our correspondence: separated by more than two hundred miles this worked in our favour. We were forced to take things slowly, which for two terrified insecure people worked out well. I started to look forward to his letters, however infrequently they appeared. It took two years (yes, two years!) for him to invite me to meet him for a coffee in London. Yes, he was prepared to travel from Cornwall to London for a coffee with me! This amazed me and terrified me at the same time. I nearly said, "No," but meet we did at Charing Cross Station. I nearly didn't recognise him because he'd had a complete change of hair style: from long hair like Meatloaf (which some of the train drivers that passed the signal box at Par used to call him) to a short back and sides that couldn't quite contain the curliness of his dark hair.

Asked by a friend the next day how it had gone, I said, "he was nicer than I remembered" – biggest understatement of my life.

My life went through a major upheaval during the period 1998 to 2000. I went from being a Primary School teacher, who attended the church I'd been born into, to a bewildered, rudderless soul.

I'd had times where I felt teaching didn't completely fit me or rather I didn't completely fit teaching. It was all I'd wanted to do since I was a child myself and I was good at it: well, I was good at explaining things; I was good at helping struggling pupils to understand concepts that were difficult for them and getting them caught up with their peers. I wasn't good at discipline: I'd come straight from college into teaching and knew nothing about life or how to play-act a person who wasn't me. I got too involved in the ups and downs going on in the lives of my pupils and got very down about it: I had never been taught how to leave things at work and not bring them home with me. It was a job that exhausted me emotionally.

I had a term out, undertaking a writing project on RE and Assessment in schools, at a college in Oxford. I will always be grateful to the Farmington Institute for the wonderful opportunity they afforded me. My time in Oxford was one of the blessings in my life: I left with a new, and now very dear, friend; I experienced new people and new broadening experiences – music, lectures, books – that I hadn't taken advantage of in my own first college experience; I tried out different churches, which widened my view of God's people and how he can be worshipped in many different ways; and it gave me a taste of something different, it suggested to me that there might be more to life than teaching.

That suggestion, that there might be more to life, reinforced the feeling that teaching might not fit me after all. At first, I thought it was just being in the same school for seven years that was causing my restlessness so decided to try somewhere new. A change in schools only made my inability to discipline more obvious and I had my confidence completely shattered by the experience. I decided to leave teaching before they asked me to go! Leaving something that I thought was my life's ambition was very hard and led to that feeling of being without a rudder.

The next few months and years, saw me in a series of odd temporary jobs: in a card factory; in WHSmith; as a steward at Hever Castle, while I undertook a writing course. Writing was something I had also been interested in as a child and teen. Eventually I got a full-time job at a conference centre: first on reception then in the conference office.

I'd been a Christian all my life, brought up in a Christian home and a member of a church I loved. I am so grateful for my Oxford experience in this area too. When an upset at my church meant that my family felt that we couldn't worship there anymore, some of the messages I'd heard while I'd visited other churches in Oxford really helped me through this time. This was another collapse of the world I knew and added to that lost feeling.

With hindsight, I see God's hand guiding me to people and places that would help me get through these trying times. I also look back now and realise that I needed to find somewhere else to worship that fit me not somewhere that suited my family so I struck out on my own and found a charismatic Anglican church to join. Having been brought up a Baptist in a church with both structure and freedom, this was a good fit. I am so grateful for the way that church family took me under their wings and encouraged me to continue growing in my faith.

So I was adrift in lots of areas in my life but having given up an all-consuming job, I actually now had time to have a long-distance relationship so I can see all the personal heartache turned out as a blessing! It still amazes me how God has used my failures and areas of weakness as strengths in later times.

After that first meeting with Tim, we began to write and email (a new form of communication to me – yes I'm that old) more frequently and met again for coffee. Four months later, I was beginning to fall for what I called 'the email person'. I was still nervous about expressing those feelings to the real person, as was he. For our next date, we decided to meet at a place half way between us: Bath. (It may be half way on a map, by train it's much easier from east to west than it is west to east but Tim didn't complain.) We had a good time together but being both as hopeless as each other we still didn't say anything about our feelings. My abiding memory, as I came away, was of him standing on the opposite railway platform to me, looking as if he wanted to hit his own head and say "Doh!" like Homer Simpson. I didn't realise it then but that was the moment we finally got in tune with each other. The next day he sent me flowers saying, "For you for being you. From me for being hopeless!"

It still took till August for us to declare our feelings! We were both hopeless! But then started a period of writing to each other once or twice a week over the next two and a half years until we got married. Those letters were so precious, each one a brick building up a strong foundation to our relationship and something that I treasure so much now.

I could go on in like vein about our love story for pages and pages but I won't. It's enough to say that we did eventually get our act together. Trains played a large part in our courtship and our fledgling relationship. I was privileged to be allowed to visit his signal box and see him at work with the old fashioned levers (which are few and far between now). Those times are some of my sweetest memories. So when were married in February 2003, it was only natural to arrange a steam train to take our guests and us to our reception and for our honeymoon to be taken on The Glacier Express through Switzerland. Happy memories!

Tim had moved jobs in 2002 so that he could move back to Devon, nearer his childhood home and his family, and had also bought a cottage in a small Mid Devon village, which I fell in love with as soon as I saw it. I still say to this day, I've fallen in love three times in my life: once with Tim; once with our cottage; and once with our village.

I also found a home in the village's small country Congregational Church: when I walked through the door the first time, I felt a wave of warm love hit me – I have never felt anything like it before or since – it was like being wrapped in an invisible hug. I felt sure that God was leading me to where he wanted me to be and where he wanted me to serve him.

During our first year of marriage, Tim lost a lot of weight and had to undergo some investigations. We feared it was cancer and were relieved when it was diagnosed as Crohn's disease. This was a known illness for us and something we assumed he would be able to find a way to live with. There was Crohn's in the family and, although that person had been very ill and had to undergo surgery at a young age, she had recovered and found a way to live a fairly normal life through medication and diet. Tim's health improved, although he had the odd blip here and there. Life went on and was good.

In 2006, we had our son which was a gift to us both. Three months later, Tim's health started to go downhill rapidly. I think the signs that something was very wrong were there earlier but I was suffering from post-natal depression and probably missed them. I wasn't the only one; I think they'd been missed by several doctors over the years.

Our last Christmas together, Tim was so ill and yet so uncomplaining. I think I was the only person who knew how much pain he was in, which was part of the problem with a diagnosis. What nobody had picked up in the past when he'd been ill in his twenties, or when he became ill during our first year of marriage was that, as well as Crohn's, he had developed an ulcer. He went into hospital in January 2007 and had several rounds of stomach surgery. Still nobody spotted the ulcer. It finally ruptured on February 12th and I lost my best friend and the love of my life.

My heart ruptured that day into a thousand tiny pieces that left half of me missing. I felt like I'd been cut in two and that I was walking around with a raw wound exposed to the world that was so obvious but only I could see. I didn't believe I could be put back together.

TWO BECOME ONE - LOSING HALF OF MYSELF

Mathew 19: 6 says "So they are no longer two, but one flesh. Therefore what God has joined together, let no one separate." This reading from Matthew's Gospel is an integral part of most Christian marriages. For us it was true. When we married we became an integrated unit: a bit like one of those Venn Diagrams you do at school – two individual bubbles, overlapping and fusing into each other. It didn't happen overnight: we made a conscious decision to talk about how to work as a partnership in marriage even before we tied the knot and, gradually over the (almost) four years of our marriage, we became a unified force.

This unity meant that when I lost Tim, half of me got ripped away. Everyone's experience will be different. I can only describe how it felt for me and that was as if I was walking around with half of my body, soul and heart missing. It actually surprised me that other people couldn't see I was a walking open and bleeding wound: it was so obvious to me. In some ways the more, I tried to get on with life the worse it felt.

In her book 'Living with Loss', Liz McNeill Taylor has a chapter entitled "The Siamese Twin Syndrome". Her description really captured what I was going through: "It is only when the widowed reach the stage of realizing that they must make a new life for themselves that they are fully conscious of what can only be described as the Siamese Twin Syndrome. This was most succinctly described for me by a woman talking about how she felt when her husband died: 'I felt as I was a Siamese twin that had lost its brother.'...This feeling of surgical cutting off is at times almost overwhelming and it affects the mind as well as the body. For my own part I really felt as if I had been split down the middle like a bit of wood...I was left with all my broken parts exposed, told to go on functioning with what was left."

Reading this was a great help as it made me realise I wasn't alone in how I was feeling. In addition to this feeling affecting mind and body, I would say it also affects the soul as well. I know the soul is individual but it is damaged by our experiences. I couldn't go to my church for three months after Tim died. I felt too raw to be in a place where my soul would be exposed while worshipping. I don't know if that makes any sense at all? But that was how I felt. The very place, that would normally comfort, was too emotional a place to go. I was fortunate that my Pastor and my church family supported me at home: being there when I needed them; leaving me alone when I wanted space. I had to go back when I was ready and not feel guilty about thinking that church was too much to bear: that feeling will pass. My adopted philosophy of "be kind to yourself" was very important here as well. Every step you take has to be when you feel ready, not when someone else tells you they think you should take it.

A few years after my own loss, I met a lady, who had just lost her husband suddenly. They had been married for forty odd years and were much older than me but she was feeling all the same things. She was crying in the churchyard and confided in me that she couldn't face going to Sunday Morning services. She sounded so guilty. I was so glad that I was able to chat to her and say that I had been through exactly the same thing and it was okay to feel that way, to give herself time and it would pass. I hope it helped. I know that she was back involved in her church life a few months afterwards.

How much can one person cry? That was a question that I asked a lot during the first few weeks. My recollection is that I cried solidly for three days straight after losing Tim then I went into a numb existence where I felt as if I was walking around in fog. I became completely obsessed with the funeral arrangements, desperate to make sure that Tim had a worthy tribute in the addresses given: trying to remember every single story he'd told me about his life. It was a huge responsibility but one that gave me a purpose.

After the funeral, that's when the real pain began. What can I tell you? Loss hurts. It is a pain unlike any other. I felt like my chest was in a vice most of the time. I couldn't sleep. I lost weight. My skin turned grey. I see photos now and can see how ill I looked. I remember hardly anything for about a year after the loss: I must have been functioning on auto-pilot.

What about when you can't cry? I found an entry in my journal where I wrote: "Sometimes I just lie here staring at the ceiling because I am too tired and too devastated even to think about you or cry." This was four months after Tim had passed.

My family; Tim's family; my friends from school, college and work; Tim's friends and work colleagues; my Church family were all amazing: visiting me, sending lovely messages and always on the end of a phone if I needed to talk. My parents were especially wonderful, putting their own lives on hold to help me look after a six month old baby while I was struggling to function as a human being let alone a mother. I was always at their house or they were at mine. It was a great comfort and a lovely caring thing for them to undertake.

But bereavement is a strange event: every experience is unique, every coping strategy must in some sense be an individual response although there will be commonalities. What helped me may not work for you and vice versa. And things that started out helping may not go on helping. The following are some of the experiences and feelings I went through and had to learn from. If they help you, I'm glad.

THE LOWS OF LOSS
Shouting in the Shower

As time passed, being with my family all the time did make it hard for me to admit I was having bad days as I didn't want to upset them and stir up their feelings of loss as well. Consequently, I would find myself crying and screaming in the shower where I would hope no-one could hear me. I think secret grieving is more common than people like to admit and maybe there's nothing wrong with it. A counsellor might say different. It may be better to grieve openly and share your feelings with others but, if you can't, just remember you're not the only one doing whatever form your grieving takes. Secret grieving is normal in my experience and from conversations I have since had with other widows.

Obsessive Behaviour & Thoughts

I found myself becoming obsessed with items that had been Tim's. He had a huge CD collection and I made a list of every single CD he had and the order they appeared on the CD rack in case I ever had to move them or, heaven forbid, they got knocked over. Tim had discerned some order that made sense to him musically and he now wasn't here to tell me what it was. I couldn't bear the thought of messing up his collection. This list is something I still have and every time I've moved the CD rack to decorate or move house, I have put them back in the same order. I don't think I will ever not be able to do so.

There are other things I've found myself doing compulsively but those have eased as time went on and I did find myself gradually able to let go of some of his things, knowing he would want me to be happy and not burdened with his possessions, but that has taken time. It is not easy to get rid of someone else's possessions. Sometimes in my journal, I wrote and asked his permission. It did feel at first as if I was also throwing Tim away and I just couldn't do it.

Don't let anyone force you into getting rid of stuff you're not ready to let go of. However, if you know you need to let go of something but need someone else to do it for you, ask for help. I had to get my parents to take his clothes to the charity shop for me. I couldn't do it myself but felt so much better once it was done. I know Tim was very kind and supported several charities so he would have wanted his clothes to benefit other people. I have to confess though that I still have one shirt and his leather jacket that he wore the first time I met him hanging in the wardrobe in the spare room. Maybe I should get rid of it but somehow it's comforting to have it there as it's so closely linked to a memory.

A few months on, I went through a period where I had obsessive thoughts that I couldn't break out of. Tim and I had both been big science fiction fans and I found myself obsessed with the idea of time travel: that I could go back a few years and let someone know he had an ulcer so it could be fixed. I felt somehow that he was still living in Cornwall, well and happy and if I could get back there to the time he was living in, I could bring him back to my time and we could go on with the life we were supposed to have together. Rationally, I knew it was stupid but it took a long time for that feeling and those thoughts to pass. I don't remember when it happened, just one morning I woke up and I didn't feel that way anymore.

I became obsessed with collecting photographs of Tim because I knew there couldn't be any new ones. Finding ones I hadn't seen before was both comforting and extremely painful but eventually I was just glad I had lots of extra pictures to look at that covered lots of different areas of Tim's life.

Avoiding Places

At first, I found I couldn't bear to go anywhere that reminded me of our courtship, wedding or life together. I avoided places where we had gone for meals or taken walks together. Near my parents' house was the preserve railway where we took our train ride to our wedding venue. It's also right next door to a supermarket that's convenient and a garden centre. When I was visiting my parents in June 2007, I decided to go to the garden centre and just to try avoid looking at the preserve line.

I saw two preserve diesel trains that would have had Tim rushing for his camera and for a moment, I thought I must text Tim then realised of course that I couldn't. Instead I text two of his friends who I knew would be interested. One of them text back to say that he had seen some diesels a couple of days before and thought, "I must email Tim". It was comforting to know that I wasn't the only one who had those momentary memory losses and then sad realisations.

After a couple of years, I went the opposite way: wanting to revisit places we had been to try to recapture the memories. I don't know whether that's something other people do or whether it's just me.

If I was going to a place I had been before with Tim, one thing that I found helpful was to take someone else with me. This way, we and my son could make new memories that were now ours and not tied to the past.

Accepting Help but Ignoring Those that "mean well"

One of the things I was most blessed by was two acquaintances who I had hardly known before Tim's death. They stepped in and talked to me about their own experiences of loss. One was a work colleague in another office in the north of the country; the other an elderly lady who had lost her first husband at a very young age and had been happily married to her second husband for nearly fifty years.

The work colleague, I'd met once. I'd emailed her with work related stuff a couple of times. She didn't know me, she didn't have to reach out but she did. She rang me at home out of the blue and I nearly didn't speak to her but I was so glad I did: hearing her story of losing her husband suddenly and also at a young age really helped me. She told me to be "kind to myself" and as time went on that became an important part of the grieving process for me and a piece of advice I still use and pass on. She also rang me two months after the funeral to see how I was getting on. In my journal, I noted I said to her: "Okay so this is it. What am I supposed to do now?"

I was lost, my life plan was shot to pieces and I didn't know how I was supposed to go on with life. My friend didn't have the answers but she reassured me my feelings were normal and I would find a way to make a new path.

The church acquaintance was able to bring a Christian's perspective to the whole ordeal which was something I desperately needed. What struck me on our first meeting was that although she was very happy and had a lovely long marriage with her second husband, she still had tears in her eyes when she spoke about her first husband. This might strike some people as being a depressing thought: that you can never get over such a loss but that wasn't what it meant to me. To me it showed that what I was going through was huge, that she understood and that I could trust her assurances that I would never forget it but that the loss would become bearable. She told me that people have two reactions to a bereavement: turning inward or turning outward. She said: that people who turn inward become bitter and hard and I have met a few of those since; that people who turn outward, find they can be both blessed by and a blessing to other people. I've met these type of people as well and it's what I determined I would try to do myself.

The people who "mean well". Not every person's story will help you. Not every person who volunteers a message to comfort will be what you need. You have to sift through the rubbish advice and catchphrases from those that "mean well" and cling on to the people who know what it's really like and whose experience resonates with you.

I relied heavily on my family, Tim's family and my close friends all of whom were quick to listen and not to speak. If you're counselling someone with loss, remember the old saying we have two ears and one mouth. Sometimes the person grieving just needs to talk or vent. They don't always want you jumping in to fix what is for them an unfixable problem.

Sometimes other people can be thoughtless. It's not personal: they just don't get what you're going through. Try to not take it personally!

About five years after Tim died, I was just coming out of the churchyard after placing flowers and a Christmas wreath on Tim's grave. I met a lady coming the other way who commented on the windy weather we were having and mentioned that she thought it was silly of people to put flowers on graves when they were just going to get blown all over the place. She said something about it being a waste of money. This was a usually kind person, an older lady, a practising Christian, but she just didn't get it. I was furious and hurt but said something polite and walked away as fast as I could. When I'd calmed down, I realised that I should just be glad for her that she was happily married for many years and had not been through what I had.

For me, buying the flowers and laying the Christmas wreath was hugely significant and still is. Tim was no longer where I could see him but this was something I could do to let him know that I still love him. It's the only present I can now give him.

Saying Goodbye

One thing I have never talked about to anyone is being faced with the body of my loved one. This is a traumatic experience on many levels. My brain seemed to split in two at the time: one half completely shut down and couldn't take in what was happening but recorded what I saw and replayed it later; the other half was talking to me and saying: "The advice from every TV programme you've ever seen is that you need to go in and say goodbye."

I was glad on one level that I got to say goodbye. It wasn't frightening, it was just surreal but it also let me know Tim wasn't there: his 'spirit' was clearly gone. After the funeral, I found that I couldn't stop seeing the scene and it was very upsetting. It took a long time to forget and remember Tim as he had been when he was alive. I believe that is a common occurrence and I just had to try every day to remember who he had been and not what he looked like the last time I saw him. Eventually the good memories reasserted themselves and the images melted away. For me, this took at least six months to a year.

I was fortunate that I had been with Tim, earlier in the afternoon and evening before he died. Immediately after losing him, I was very angry with myself for going home when I did. I think part of me knew that he was really unwell and something might go wrong but much later I saw this as a blessing from God. I'm sure he blocked the immediacy of the danger from my mind so that I went home, got the call to say things were not going well and was able to ask my Pastor and his wife to take me back to the hospital. It was well after eleven when we got there and we had to wait outside ICU for some time before someone came to see us and break the news that Tim was gone. Like I said I remembered my brain recording what was going on but I went into complete shock. Much later, I remembered the ICU Head Nurse crying as he told me the news; being told that the last thing Tim spoke about was about me and our son (which much later was very comforting); hearing my Pastor and his wife pray for Tim was very important for me as a Christian and was especially important to be able to tell Tim's father, who was Roman Catholic, that he had had prayer surrounding him as he died. I would never have been able to drive home in the state I was in so it was a blessing that I had people with me.

However, because I did not see him as he died, I felt for a while that I hadn't been able to say goodbye to him properly. I found the books: "I Wasn't Ready to Say Goodbye: Surviving, Coping, and Healing after the Sudden Death of a Loved One" by Noel Brook and Pamela D Blair and "Praying Our Goodbyes" by Joyce Rupp (1998) very helpful. Rupp's book is not only about losing a loved one, it is about all sorts of things that we can suffer loss over. I found it really useful to take her advice and pray through what I was going through and using prayer to help me say goodbye. I have also used that technique since to get over thwarted ambitions!

Much later I came to realise, that the fact that the whole last month of Tim's life was spent in the hospital became a blessing – I will come back to this later.

Trying to be Two People

One of the things that has been a blessing to me is my son. At first, he was the only reason I got out of bed - because I had to - but as time passed each day got less painful and I was able to deal with each day a little better than the last. It takes as long as it takes and, to be perfectly honest, I don't think I remember much of the period of his life from six months to eighteen months (apart from a few highlights, of course, like him learning to walk at ten months) because I was just existing on auto-pilot.

Having a child is also something that can trigger a lot of lows because all the things that should be shared highlights are now yours alone. I found that very hard to begin with and do still have moments now.

There is also the desperate feeling that to make his life whole, I needed to try to be both a father and a mother. I didn't feel I was doing a good job of either to start with because, obviously, I wasn't his Dad and, secondly, half of me was missing so I wasn't even a whole Mum. I still struggle with making decisions on my own but I guess any single parent has that problem, it's not just confined to widowhood.

At some point, I realised I was wearing myself out trying to be two people and had to settle for just trying to rebuild enough of me to be one whole parent. I would say that it took a few years to accept that I was just one person and it would have to be enough.

Broken

I think that I am broken:
Like eggshells hitting concrete
Or a glass mirror splitting;
Bad luck pooling at at my feet.

I think that I am broken:
Like a clock with faulty gears,
Strings snapped on a guitar,
Music silenced by my tears.

I think that I am broken:
Like promises made then lost.
My hopes in shattered pieces,
My heart buffeted and tossed.

Can broken dreams be mended?
Can a heart reset, regrow?
Can a life find new direction?
Can I heal? I do not know.

Your grace is my salvation,
Your caring makes me whole.
Gluing my fractured psyche
And mending my broken soul.

For You are the great Healer
To comfort Your dearest wish

And all I know is you're here, my Lord,
And your love is the greatest gift.

IT'S ALL RIGHT TO BE SELFISH

As a Christian from a Christian family, I was brought up to believe in and practise JOY – Jesus first, Others second and Yourself last. I still believe it's a good way to live most of the time. It's also good guidance for serving people like Jesus did. But as a widow, I've had to learn that it is okay for me to be selfish sometimes.

Accepting that I would have bad days, where I needed to either be alone or do something just for me, was a steep learning curve but very necessary in my journey to wholeness. Understanding that I was allowed to do and find things that made me feel happy or places that made me feel peaceful when I needed to, was an important part of helping me glue myself back together.

I just had to be selfish sometimes and do what I needed to do - not what I thought other people wanted me to do – to take care of my own mental health.

I couldn't share the anniversary of Tim's passing for the first few years: I had to go and hide in a hole by myself and leave other people to sort themselves and their own grief out. That was okay. It was what I needed to do to stay sane.

The first Christmas without him, I asked all my side of the family to go away with me for Christmas so that my son would have a good family time and because I couldn't face having anything to do with Christmas in our home. It was incredibly selfish of me. It cost them time and money. It probably looked mean to Tim's side of the family but I just had to do it for me.

I still feel bad that I don't ever spend Christmas Day with Tim's side of the family but I still can't.

Don't get me wrong. I did not stop being part of their family. They are as dear to me as the people I grew up with. I always see them before or after Christmas or spend New Year with them. My son and I saw them and still see them at least once a month. They have been a huge part of keeping my memories of Tim alive and helping me to pass on the truth of who he really was to our son. I wouldn't be without them and I needed them as much as they needed us to help each other grieve but in this one thing I had to be selfish: I don't know why I can't do Christmas Day when other anniversaries and occasions have become so much easier to share. I've had to simply accept that it is that way and I just hope that they can understand and forgive me.

WHEN TO STOP SHARING YOUR GRIEF

Does there come a point when you should stop talking about how rubbish you're feeling? Do you need to tell everyone you meet what you've been through?

This was a tricky area for me. For a while, I wanted to blurt out to every new person I met that I had lost Tim. I think it was because, as I mentioned previously, I felt like I was a walking open wound and almost wanted to explain to people why I looked like that...even though they couldn't see it! Of course, it's essential to find people you can share with on the bad days and talking is an essential part of recovery but I think you have to be careful not to get stuck in a wallowing mode.

I certainly had to learn to 'look up' and focus on God to get a wider perspective of this world and I had to 'look outwards' to remember that I am not the only person in this world who is hurting and maybe I could help others and so help myself in the process.

One of the books, I found helpful through my journey through grief was by Fiona Castle, widow of Roy Castle, the much loved presenter during my childhood of "Record Breakers" (amongst other things). She has certainly learned how to look up and out. In her anthology, "His Light in Our Darkness", she writes:

In my own case I decided I had a choice. I could either be miserable because people were not   caring enough and therefore not meeting all my needs, or I could choose to be cheerful and save my tears for the bedroom behind closed doors. I realised I didn't need to burden anyone else with my

*grief – it was between me and God only and I didn't want
them to reject me because of my constant misery!*

She also quoted there a piece by an anonymous writer,
which says:

> *Tears are proof of love*
> *The more love, the more tears*
> *If this be true, then how could*
> *we ask that the pain cease*
> *Altogether?*
> *For then memory of love would go with it*
> *The pain of grief is the price we pay for love.*

In her book, Fiona Castle also quotes another anonymous
piece, "Beatitudes for those who Comfort". Sage advice for
anyone trying to comfort someone who is experiencing grief
and words that I try to follow now that I am further on in my
own journey and trying to be the one who is doing the
comforting:

Beatitudes for Those Who Comfort

Blessed are *those who do not use tears to measure the true
feelings of others.*
Blessed are *those who stifle the urge to say, 'I understand' –
when they don't.*
Blessed are *those who do not expect the bereaved to put into
the past someone who is still fresh in their hearts.*
Blessed are *those who do not always have a quick
comforting" answer.*

Blessed are those who do not make judgments on another's closeness to God by their reaction to the loss of their loved one.

Blessed are those who hear with their hearts and not with their minds.

Blessed are those who allow the sorrowing enough time to heal.

Blessed are those who admit their discomfort and put it aside to help others.

Blessed are those who do not give unwanted advice.

Blessed are those who continue to call, visit and reach out when the crowd has dwindled and the wounded are left standing alone.

Blessed are those who know the worth of each person as a unique individual and do not pretend that they can be replaced or forgotten.

Blessed are those who realize the fragility of sorrow and handle it with an understanding shoulder and a loving heart.

KEEPING A JOURNAL

I've always been a person who can only express deeper thoughts in the written word so for me the idea of keeping a journal was perfectly natural, even more so in this case as I basically decided to carry on writing love letters to Tim because that had been such a strong part of our courtship.

In coming to write this book, I opened my journal for the first time in years. Tim died on 12th February 2007. I started my journal on 1st March of that year. I wrote in it when I needed to. Looking at it now, I can see I wrote two or three times a week from March until the end of July, then it dropped to roughly once a week from August to December. Quicker than could be believed, the first anniversary came round and that hit me hard. I can see I went back to writing two to three times a week from February 2008 through to May then gradually my entries eased off to roughly once a week again. I wrote randomly for the rest of 2008 and in the next two years, mostly related to events, birthdays, and anniversaries. My last entry is May 2011. That last entry is significant to me for lots of reasons:

1) It took four years for me to not need to write to Tim! Give yourself time. You've been through a monumental experience that has left deep scars. Like any physical injury, recovery is individual, it will take as long as it takes for the wound to scab over and for you to be able to get moving again.

2) In my last journal entry, I wrote "Since your birthday this year, I've been trying to talk naturally about you in front of Thomas and now I've talked to your

nephew and your sisters about it, they feel they can
mention you too. I think that's good for us all."
It took me four years to realise that everyone in
Tim's family was taking their cue from me as to
whether they could talk about their brother, their
uncle, their son. I had to give them permission to talk
about him without wincing. He wouldn't have
wanted people walking on eggshells because of him
but it took time for all of us to be able to speak
without a huge black hole opening up in the room.

I decided I would include verbatim my first ever entry
here because it might be helpful to you to know that
anything you feel; anything you want to express is okay. It
also shows the things that were on my mind as a Christian.
These are thoughts that you don't have to think about if you
don't believe. Sometimes believing is an added burden as
well as a blessing.

Thursday 1ˢᵗ March 2007

My Darling Tim

I miss you so much every day. I don't know how often
you're allowed to see what's going on down here on Earth or
whether you will ever hear when I talk to you but I thought I
would write to you every day so you know how things are
going and how your 'little boy' is doing.

Pip (my grandfather) used to talk to Nana and he was the
most secure committed Christian I ever knew so if he thought
that she could still see him/hear him somehow, I hope that
the same is true for us.

I can still feel you in my heart: that bit of you that completed me when we fell in love and realised that it was forever.

At the funeral on Monday when Canon M was praying for you, just before we were about to leave the church for the committal of your body, I had this sense of peace come over me and this strong conviction that you weren't there but were safely in heaven. That's the hope that's keeping me going: that one day we will be reunited. I'm not sure I can wait 40 minutes, let alone 40 years – I was never very patient as you well know – but I'll try to hang on, love. Oh how I long to see you and hear your soft giggle and gentle voice.

I went to see Auntie M today – it was hard and we both cried. She's so sad that you're gone and sad for me, plus of course her friend V has just died and her great niece (my first cousin) died on 23rd. Auntie M still misses Uncle R and she talked about him. She said she didn't know how people without faith keep going and we must both hang on to the promises of hope. She had "In Heavenly Love Abiding" for Uncle R's funeral – it's one of her favourites – and used that phrase in the memorial book for him at the crematorium.

T was so sweet today. I took him to feed the ducks – it was hard because that's what you and I did with him when we were here at New Year but it was a lovely day and he enjoyed it. He's been whizzing up and down the corridor here – he doesn't have that much room at home so he's loving it!

I popped in to town tonight to get this journal and some books for T. I bought the train one that I told you about a few weeks ago. It's a steam train again but it does show a level crossing and the train leaving the station. I think he'll love it when he's a bit bigger.

I nearly cried in WHSmith's because there were cards with 'wife' on and I know that I'll never get another card from you. Also I bought a mother's day card for my mother and then realised I'd better get one for yours as you can't anymore. Your poor Mum.

I keep waiting for the end of this parallel universe episode to come to an end and for me to return to the universe I should be in but it's real unfortunately...I live in a world which no longer has you in it. It's agony.

I need to sleep. I'll write again tomorrow.

There are themes here in this first entry that recur through my journal and recur through my life.

1) My grandfather. Pip, was a massive influence in my life, and in my Christian life, and I was always pleased that he had the opportunity to meet Tim. He sadly left us when I'd been going out with Tim for two months and had said something lovely to me one of the last times I visited him: he said he liked Tim. I said I was very lucky. He looked at me with the twinkle in his eye that he used to get and said, "He's very lucky." For someone who didn't believe they deserved anyone to like them, that was amazing!

2) Auntie M. After my grandmother died, when she was only young, Auntie M (her sister) became an integral part of our family, filling the grandparent void a little for my brother and I and particularly for my younger

sisters who only knew her. She married in her thirties, she was a teacher, she was a Christian, she was widowed young. She became the person who I most identified with and she identified with me. She shared things about Uncle R that she hadn't told other members of the family because they weren't working from the same script as we were. She had always had a lovely wooden robin that she kept close to her bed in her residential home. Visiting her one time after Tim's passing, she told me that she'd bought it for herself the first Christmas after Uncle R passed as she knew he would have bought her something simple but lovely and she felt he would approve. Ever since I have treated myself to a little something for Christmas on Tim's behalf. As I mentioned, "In Heavenly Love Abounding" was a recurring motif for Auntie M and it became mine too. I had it etched into Tim's gravestone as it summed up my hope that he was safely in heaven with Pip and that I would be reunited with him in the next life.

LOOKING FOR ANSWERS FROM GOD – THE WHY AND THE HOW COULD YOU?

I was very, very angry with God for not answering my prayers and those of all the good Christian folk around me who prayed faithfully for Tim's recovery. I felt I'd been cheated by Him. Tim and I had waited so long to find each other: it didn't seem fair to get such a short time together. I felt I was trying to be a faithful servant and follow God's teaching and do what God wanted me to do. Why had he let this happen? I'm afraid God had to put up with a lot of ranting and venting for weeks and months afterwards. Thankfully, he has broad shoulders!

Worse than anger in some ways was that I felt disillusioned and let down, as if God had broken a promise he'd given me. But gradually, I returned to Isaiah 43 and God's promise to me. He had never promised that I wouldn't go through floods or fire, he only promised that he would be with me and that they wouldn't overwhelm me completely.

I found my grandfather's journal (written after he lost his wife of sixty years) a great comfort. He was a devout Christian yet he had the same questions, he felt the same pain, he found comfort in the words of others. Some of the words that he had copied down really spoke to me and gave me hope. These are all extracts from Catherine Marshall's book 'To Live Again' which he found particularly meaningful:

"God does not reduce the problem. He builds up the resources."

"Can I actually really think that God, who cried, led, provided, protected and united us as one for 42 years, would desert us in such a basic experience as death?"

"Grief is a real wound, a mutilation, a gaping hole in the human spirit – God alone can finally heal a broken heart."

"If our loved ones are with the Lord and He is with us 'all the days until the end of the age', we can't be far apart from each other!"

My grandfather had also found comfort in Isaiah 43 and as you can imagine this leapt off the page at me:

"When you pass through the water I will be with you; and thro' the rivers, they shall not overflow you....For I am the Lord God, the Holy One. Isaiah 43 v 1-3

L Weatherhead's comment:

"God does not say 'I will excuse you from the waters: I will show you a short cut by which you may escape the rivers'... God does say 'In all experiences through which you have to pass, I shall be there too.' Thus shall the experiences which cannot be called anything but evil, the experiences I have hated and from which I have shrunk, be woven into a pattern of good and made to serve the purposes of a holy, loving wise and omnipotent God."

This really helped me to cling onto God's promises to me but I did still feel as if I couldn't hear God's voice for a long time. I felt like I was screaming at him across a huge chasm through a wall of thick ice: so thick and opaque that he couldn't hear me and I couldn't see or hear him. I can't say I even felt that he was with me but I stubbornly clung on to what I had always believed: that even if I couldn't feel it, he was there.

I am in good company with these feelings: in Psalm 13, David writes-

> How long, LORD? Will you forget me forever?
> How long will you hide your face from me?
> How long must I wrestle with my thoughts
> And day after day have sorrow in my heart?
> ...But I trust in your unfailing love,
> My heart rejoices in your salvation.

I realised from something I wrote in July 2019, that I was finally able to accept that God doesn't always step in:

In Exodus chapter 20 verses 3-7, God speaks to Moses saying "You shall have no other gods before me...You shall not bow down to them (other gods) or worship them..." and through reading and watching the story of Daniel with my teen church group, we saw how this commandment could have cost Daniel and his three friends their lives on more than one occasion. Instead, they remained faithful even when facing certain death and God rewarded their faithfulness by stepping in to keep them healthy, literally stepping in to stand alongside them in the middle of what should have been a fiery death, and keeping the lions' mouths shut so that Daniel wouldn't be eaten.

The book of Daniel is an amazing read and one that can be a source of great inspiration. God doesn't often step in physically and save us but we can be sure that, even when he doesn't, he's right alongside us in the fire, keeping our souls safe and will reward our faithfulness to Him.

As the ice melted over time, it
that God was there and He was w
also kept my soul safe.

God understands loss. In som
to a non-believer, He has been t
been through. For one brief sec
cut off from him and He was cu
loss. He absorbed it into His m

I know God is Unchanging I
Unchangeable. Theologians have many ,
on this subject. I don't know who's right and, obviously, . _
no theologian. I won't know until I get to heaven and can ask
the question but to me God has to have been changed by the
cross or nothing makes sense.

s, even though I felt like crying most of the
were instances that made me smile as well as cry.
ber vividly when I had to call our electrician round to
mething just two months after Tim had died. I felt
mpelled to tell him what had happened. He swore
vehemently! A little while later, he came up to me and said,
"He was a lovely chap." Both expressions really moved me.
He was a 'rough diamond' sort of person and the fact that he
was so shocked and that he was then able to say something
so sweet was a real comfort to me.

I mentioned earlier that the last month of Tim's life was
spent in hospital. At the time it was an awful, worrying time
but sometime later, those days became a comfort and a
blessing to me.

During that enforced still time together, we had the
chance to talk, to pray together, to express our love for each
other and talk about our son. Some of those conversations
became a great source of comfort and, even though initially I
felt I hadn't said goodbye, I soon realised that we had spent a
whole month re-affirming how much we loved each other. I
came to realise that I was much more fortunate than some
people - who have a loved one snatched away unexpectedly.

FIGHTING THE FOG

I find the month of February very difficult. The first few years after Tim passed, what I can only describe as a fog would descend on me in mid-November and carry on until March. After three or four years, the fog began in December then it moved to starting after Christmas. Now, it tends to be just the whole of February as this month contains the Anniversary, Valentine's Day and our Wedding Anniversary. I usually feel as if I am walking through treacle, trying to get my thoughts to take some coherent form. I've realised (only in the last three years!) that it helps if I acknowledge that that is how I'm feeling and tell someone: not so that they can fix me but just so I can get it out in the open and somehow saying it out loud or in a text/message helps to push the fog back a little.

I have blips when it's my birthday or Tim's birthday – usually the day before is worse – then I'm okay again.

Don't be surprised if something comes out of the blue and side swipes you. During the ninth year, I felt pretty good and thought I was finally moving on. The tenth year hit me like a ton of bricks and I went back to feeling rubbish for two months. I think what made it worse was friends were celebrating ten year wedding anniversaries. Just one of those things. The next year was easier.

During this period, I try to be kind to myself, get lots of sleep and don't try to do too much. I try not to make any major decisions during the fog times otherwise, when my brain's working again, I wonder why I've done certain things!

THE LIFE AFTER THIS ONE

As Christians we are supposed to believe in an afterlife.

I do. But it's not that simple. This belief raises more questions, such as:

Do we go straight to heaven? Jesus told the robber on the cross that he would be with him in Paradise that day. If you're a scholar, you'll tell me the Greek word for Paradise means something different from heaven anyway.

Is time different in heaven? Will our consciousness wake up at the end times and we'll all be in heaven at the same time? Do we sleep then go to heaven like the prophet Samuel in the Old Testament (although I have a whole other raft of questions and thoughts about that!)?

Are Catholics right? Do we go through purgatory to burn off all our impurities before we enter heaven?

Can we be like neutrinos? In two places at the same time - safely in heaven and also able to visit earth?

I can only give you anecdotal instances that have comforted me. I don't know whether the occurrence was actually an angel or whether it was the person in question. I only know in my own case, it definitely felt like Tim.

1)   My father-in-law saw Tim standing at the end of his bed the night he died and he told me the time of his passing before I was able to say anything. He wasn't sure if he was fully awake or not but it was a peaceful experience.

2)   Three months after Tim passed, I was driving alone in my car and I felt something next to me and smelt him and felt very peaceful. In counselling with my doctor two

weeks later, I mentioned this occurrence, fully expecting her to tell me I was mad and she relayed that she was also counselling another older lady who had lost her husband and she had had the same experience. I then mentioned it to a family member who had sensed her father and smelt him a few weeks after he passed.

3) Two family members had very vivid dreams about Tim where he gave messages to them. I have heard of other people (Christian and non-Christian) having this happen.

4) Over the following year, I smelt Tim a couple of other times when I was visiting the churchyard.

5) Two and a half years after losing Tim, I felt him near me again. I was Christmas shopping and I felt as if he was next to me looking at what I was buying and approving my choices. I can't explain it any other way.

6) My last and most vivid experience was on Christmas Day 2010. I was really down that day, went along to a local church with my parents as we always go to church Christmas morning in our family. I sat down in a row with one space next to me. I was praying and saying how much I was missing Tim when suddenly I felt someone sit down next to me and my whole right side felt intensely warm as if someone was sitting right up close to me. It felt like a hug and was very peaceful and comforting. To me, it felt like Tim.

TURNING OUTWARDS

For my 21st birthday, my grandfather gave me a collection of Rudyard Kipling poems because I'd always loved the poems "The Way Through The Woods" and "The Thousandth Man" and wanted to read more. On the inside cover, he wrote: "May you ever 'find some needful job that's crying to be done'", which is a quotation from "The Glory of the Garden".

I have always tried to be a person who helped others but, after Tim died, I came back to this inspiration of Pip's and tried to make it my motto and do what my elderly lady friend had wisely advised me to do: turn outwards.

I got involved in my local toddler group and ended up running it. Then a little while later, I also started another one with a friend, which was the culmination of a vision I felt I had been given before my son was even a thought in my mind that God wanted me working with mothers and toddlers. The friend had the same heart for starting a group at our church, which had no young children and, with her as a driving force, the "Springers" group was born.

When my son started pre-school, the committee that ran it had all just left so I was roped in. That became both a blessing and a curse. It took up a lot of time and energy, particularly as a little while after I joined some financial irregularities came to light and the whole organisation nearly fell apart but I had a good team of mothers working alongside me and we managed to pull it back and get it going stronger than before. It's now become part of our local school system and is still going strong.

I was proud of what I achieved but had to be careful not to keep saying yes to things. Learning to be a Mary and not a Martha (see Luke 10: 38-39). My grandfather would not have wanted me to run myself into the ground just to be a useful servant. This aspect of learning to "listen and to be still" and to "not be doing all the time" is something that I have always struggled with.

I found the book "Having a Mary Heart in a Martha World" by Joanna Weaver very helpful and have read it several times. Every time I find myself doing too much and feeling burned out, I reach for her book and realign my thinking.

Keeping busy is good but don't use it as a way to ignore all the healing that your heart, mind and soul needs to go through to get you back to a whole person.

I also try to remember that Tim would often stop me when he felt I'd been doing too much. He would step into view and say, "You've done enough. Sit down and have a cup of tea." Now, his voice appears in my head when it's time to take a break and just 'be'.

I think the good thing about turning outwards, and trying to serve people, is it reminds me of my own blessings and the good things I have in my life when others may be struggling. I always think it's good just to be able to make the world a tiny bit better than it was when I found it.

Sometimes, even though I want to serve God, I don't feel like I have the energy. I have gone through periods when I feel as if I am barely hanging on by my fingernails: usually in February or when I am 'fighting the fog'. I feel like saying, "I canna do it, Captain. There's no more power!" to misquote Scotty in Star Trek, but that's because I have forgotten, I'm not supposed to supply the power. That's God's job. He is the power source for everything he wants done in this world. I just need to listen out for his instructions and work with the rest of the crew to get the ship moving.

Psalm 61 shows David calling out to God "as my heart grows faint". I'm sure we've all experienced that feeling at one time or another. When David feels at the end of his trust and his strength, he remembers two things: one that God is a rock; and two that God shelters us under his wings. These are amazing pictures that have really helped me to trust in God and remember that he is there for me.

When I studied John's Gospel for my A Level RE, I remember reading the idea of the "dual contradiction": two things that seem totally opposite in human terms and therefore cannot co-exist, but in God these two things hold together at the same time. God is love but hates evil; God is All-Powerful but allows free will; God is both a rock (solid, forbidding, strong) and a mother hen (soft, warm and welcoming).

When we comprehend God's amazing capacity to be just what we need in any given circumstance, we can say with David, "Then will I sing praise to your name and fulfil my vows day after day."

So now I try to remember to ask God for strength and trust that he will supply the power I need. It helps to remember how big God is: bigger than we can comprehend; able to do more than I could ever think of asking Him.

Design Not Chance

Frosty fractals on a cold window pane
Hexagonal points of snowflakes, falling
Pentagonal stars in a primrose heart
Glistening white snowdrops with heads drooping
A robin soaring as it sings its praise
For the colours of a new born spring day

Design not chance has created wonders!

Raindrops creating circles in a pond
Ferns, in between mossy rocks, unfurling
The hoot of an owl in a moonlit sky
The symmetry of a butterfly's wings
A wren's circular nest, spider's web spun
Wild miniature strawberries in the sun

Design not chance has created wonders!

Humpback whales arcing above the ocean
Snowy mountains reflect in crystal lakes
Sunlight dancing through myriad green leaves
Oak trees, Silver Birch and red-barked Maples
Fields of poppies, harvest mouse climbing wheat
Bluebell carpets laid between silent trees

Design not chance has created wonders!

Honeycomb hexagons dripping sweetly
Rainbows arching over darkening moors
Light separating through a glass prism
The ordered chaos of solar systems
Perfectly formed DNA helix strands
Patterns in numbers, the nine times table

Design not chance has created wonders!

Friendship and love, family connection,
Ten tiny fingers and ten tiny toes
That heart shaped space between two loving souls

Design not chance has created wonders!
Sing of God's greatness to the highest heights!

FALLING IN LOVE WITH GOD AGAIN

As I said earlier, for a long time I was just clinging onto the cliff face but gradually I started to move on again in my journey with God. I tried to join in with bible studies when I could and learn from more mature Christians about their walks with God.

I became a deacon at my church in June 2015. One of the duties involves writing a little piece for our monthly newsletter on a rota basis.

When researching ideas to help me come up with something to write, I have come across a few gems that have helped me in my walk and through the journey from loss to living.

In July 2018, I wrote:

My bible reading notes this month have been written by Gill Beard and I have found myself having to stop and think several times as I read her thoughts on what it means to be commissioned by God. I found her song "Now is the time" particularly challenging.

'Trusting in you to guide me forward on your path'
(Excerpt from "Now Is The Time" by Gill Beard © 1989)
We are all at varying stages on our walks with God and so different phrases and verses of this song may have jumped out at you from the ones that caught my attention. I found the second verse made me stop and think. I'm not sure I always find it easy to trust where God is leading especially if it feels like he's asking me to step out into a place that's not well signposted, maybe even a little foggy so that I can only

see a few steps ahead at a time. Personally, I would like to see the whole map from start to finish!

One thing about a foggy path is it means you have to trust the person who is leading you. "Trust in the LORD with all your heart and lean not on your own understanding: in all your ways acknowledge him, and he will make your paths straight." Proverbs 3: 5-6

As we learn to trust and step out where God leads, we will hopefully find that the journey is rewarding and the destination is better than we could have ever imagined.

In January 2019, I wrote:

Isaiah 40 verses 1, 9-11:
Comfort, comfort my people,
says your God.
You who bring good news to Zion,
go up high on a mountain.
You who bring good news to Jerusalem,
lift up your voice with a shout,
lift it up, do not be afraid;
say to the towns of Judah, 'Here is your God!'
See the Sovereign LORD comes with power,
and he rules with a mighty arm...
He tends his flock like a shepherd;
he gathers the lambs in his arms
and carries them close to his heart;
he gently leads those that have young.

I hope as you read this that you will have had a happy and blessed time at Christmas, sharing the season of goodwill with family and friends.

However, I know that many in our church family and local community have found the last few weeks of 2018 a hard, difficult and sad time. Many have struggled with illness and with loss. The news has been full of uncertainty and daily reminders of humankind's falling short of God's plans for us.

At times like these, I'm glad that I have a Father in heaven who understands my pain: that he sent his Son to live amongst us a child and an adult to fully experience life in all its ups and downs; that somehow, despite everything he is alongside me sharing and guiding.

I hope that the image that Isaiah paints of the shepherd holding the lambs close to his heart brings some comfort to all of us. What a lovely picture of a loving, tender parent who cares deeply for us and wants to hold us close. As we face the uncertainties of 2019, I hope we can all hold on to the thought that we are being carried close to God's heart and he will gently lead us in the weeks and months that lie ahead.

In April 2019, I wrote this:

♪ *Hallelujah! For the Lord our God Omnipotent reigneth. Hallelujah!*
The kingdom of this world is become the kingdom of our Lord and of His Christ. Hallelujah!

When I was at teacher training college in Canterbury, Kent, I was in the college choir and we were fortunate one year to have the opportunity to sing Handel's "Messiah" at Canterbury Cathedral. "Messiah" is a wonderful work to sing anywhere and at any time but, for me, singing in the cathedral will always be a special recollection. Particularly memorable is the moment when we reached the "Hallelujah" chorus.

I remember our Conductor telling us during practices at the college that when we got to the pause in the last phrase, he would hold us silent for a couple of seconds longer than was usually necessary and that we must watch him like hawks and not start singing again until he indicated.

The day came and we were all filled with the nervous excitement that goes with any sort of performance and all keyed up ready for the pause. What a moment it was! The Hallelujahs built up to a huge crescendo and then silence. As we and the audience listened, the sound of our voices ran down the entire length of the cathedral like a wave...then a final rousing Hallelujah! I got goose bumps then and I get goose bumps now just thinking about it! It was   an amazingly uplifting moment: for a second or two, it was as if earthly praise was rising up and colliding with the adoration of angels.

What is the work "Messiah" celebrating if not the amazing wonderful resurrection of Jesus? God sent his own Son to be our Christ (Saviour), to make a bridge between us and God so that we could have a relationship with Him. In John 3: 16, we read, "For God so loved the world that he gave his one and only Son that whoever believes in him shall not perish but have eternal life."

The knowledge that God cared enough about us to send Jesus, that Jesus cared enough about us to sacrifice his life for us should make us rise to our feet and sing Hallelujah!

At some point every Easter time, I try to listen to the Messiah to remind myself through the words and music of the incredible love God has for us and to be thankful. I hope that this Easter will be a time of thanksgiving for all of us and an opportunity to reflect on God's love and marvel at how much he loves each and every one of us.

Hallelujah! Happy Easter!

Looking at this now, I can see that I am back in love with God and able to marvel again at how much he loves me!

In October 2019, I wrote this letter to my church which was deeply personal but liberating on so many levels and was an opportunity to thank all those people who had helped me through my bereavement and to acknowledge God's love for me:

"For God so loved the world that he gave his one and only Son, that whoever believes in him shall not perish but have eternal life. For God did not send his Son into the world to condemn the world, but to save the world through him."
(John 3: 16-17)

Dear Friends,

I've been thinking a lot recently about what it means for each one of us to be loved by God and keep coming back to John's Gospel and the verses printed above.

I grew up in a loving Christian home, where Christian beliefs and values were taught and acted out so I am more fortunate than many of the people who live and work around me. When I was eleven, I realised that I wanted to own for myself the faith I had been taught as a child so I decided to ask Jesus to come into my life. That day was the beginning of a journey, which I am still on, to try to better understand God's love, Jesus's strength and the Holy Spirit's guidance.

I "knew" God loved me from childhood because that was what I had been taught but I think it took me until I was in my twenties to really acknowledge and understand the sacrificial and gracious love of God: that He would allow his Son to die for my sins and, although nothing I could ever give Him would be of the same value as Jesus' life, He actually delights in my praise, my gratitude and my pitiful attempts to serve the world in which He has placed me.

In my thirties, I married Tim and we settled in our village where I found the local Congregational Church and all its lovely members. I remember feeling a warm blanket of love surround me the first time I walked through the door. The kindness of those dear members (some of whom have passed away now) were one part of the loving support that helped me through the sudden and shattering loss of my husband. Thank you to all of you.

I struggled for a long time with how such a thing could happen. Like many people who face suffering or bereavement, I asked the questions why and how could God let it happen?

I do not believe God chooses to cause pain, death or suffering. I firmly believe that God is a God of Love and suffers alongside His children when they are hurting. I believe God is in control and yet has to allow bad things to happen because he operates the world on the basis of free will.

From my own very personal experience, I can say that although I couldn't hear God's voice in the throes of grief, I could feel the strong arms of Jesus surrounding me and keeping me upright when all I wanted to do was curl up in a ball.

As I have carried on with my walk, I have learned a great deal from that experience. I think I've learned to be more patient, more understanding and more committed to showing God's love to the world.

I can see that this letter was a forerunner to this book!

Recently, I have found that two songs, by the US band 'Mercy Me', have really spoken to me. Their song "The Hurt and The Healer" starts with the question "Why?" and sums up completely all my feelings and questions that I had for the first few years. They sing about how even though part of the singer has died, he is still alive in Jesus. Jesus is the ultimate Healer of all our wounds and hurts. What it takes me a book to write, they have managed to contain in a song! I would urge you to look it up and listen.

The second song of theirs, that has become very important to me, is "Even If". The song is based in part on the book of Daniel, which I mentioned earlier.

In Daniel 3: 16-18, it says:

"Shadrach, Meshach and Abednego replied to him, 'King Nebuchadnezzar, we do not need to defend ourselves before you in this matter. If we are thrown into the blazing furnace, the God we serve is able to deliver us from it, and he will deliver us from Your Majesty's hand. **But even if he does not**, we want you to know, Your Majesty, that we will not serve your gods or worship the image of gold you have set up.'" (My bold emphasis.)

I can finally say that I can sing this song and mean the words that say God is my hope even if...It has taken a long time to get to this place.

BELIEVING GOD'S PROMISE

During 2020, I have started trying to express my gratitude to God for all the blessings I do have in my life and some of these have taken the form of poems.

Returning to what I believe is God's promise to me (Isaiah 43 – RSV):

> "Fear not, for I have redeemed you; I have called you
> by name, you are my mine. (1b)
> When you pass through the waters I will be with you;
> and through rivers, they shall not overwhelm me;
> when you walk through fire you shall not be burned,
> and the flame shall not consume you."

I have been able to write the following poem and mean it and I hope that in some small way, this will give you hope to hang on to God's promises and that it is possible to rebuild yourself and start travelling again.

The Journey

I'm trav'lling on a journey
Don't know how long or short
I try to follow signposts
From things that I've been taught

I've travelled far already
My way's crossed flood and fire
I've lost the road completely
Been sucked down in the mire

But God he did not leave me
Stood beside me all the way
When I fell in the black abyss
He was holding me each day

His arms were wrapped around me
His hands reached out with care
His feet they showed the way back home
My pain his heart did bear

For great is God Almighty
My father and my friend
Though hard the path, I'm learning
To trust Him to the end

My journey is still going
A new path He's mapped out
And though I did not choose it
He's faithful through my doubt

For he loves me as a daughter
I'm never on my own
His angels and the saints above
Are waiting at His home

A home that he's prepared for all
Who love him to their core
He's waiting with arms open wide
By the edge of heaven's door

If we could only see it
All our doubts would fade away
But we can feel it in our hearts
When we listen to Him say:

My child, you are the dearest
The one I've longed to save
For you I held back nothing
My precious Son I gave

Lord, help me to remember
As I travel on today
That I am in your family
And heaven lights my way

SO ARE THE PIECES BACK TOGETHER?

I think the verse in my poem, The Journey, gives some sort of answer:

My journey is still going
A new path He's mapped out
And though I did not choose it
He's faithful through my doubt

I am not the same person that I was. My life is not what I expected it to be. I've lost some parts of me that I will never get back but I have rebuilt myself with new pieces and God is making something new in me. I guess the illustration that comes to my mind is that of a piece of coloured glass smashed to pieces but put back together to make a beautiful mosaic that also now has a different function from its previous one.

My last entry in my journal was in May 2011, after my youngest sister got married. Still addressing Tim in letter form, I wrote:

I suppose it's a good sign that I haven't written in here for over a year, that I don't need to grieve in this way anymore., that I've been able to accept a little more what's happened and am trying to move my life forward but always taking you with me.

I can't say that I wouldn't want to have changed what happened BUT I have accepted it. I believe all of our experiences make us who we are and we have to decide whether we use those experiences to make us stronger and put them to good use or not.

Tim will always be the best part of me: and I have been blessed and changed by knowing him. I am more than grateful for the time I had with him.

I am just also grateful that I have a loving Heavenly Father that is with me every day as I travel and that I know that He's keeping Tim safe until we are reunited.

In Heavenly Love Abiding Always.

Tim

You left:
A hole the size of the universe in my heart;
Good memories and timeless moments
etched across my life;
The best parts of you in my mind and soul.

You gave:
Your love; your friendship; your kindness;
your humour; your gentle strength; your trust;
and you gave me faith in myself

You transformed:
All my loneliness into belonging;
all my anxieties into calm;
and all my lack of self-confidence into self-assurance.

You shared:
Your family; your friends; your hopes; your dreams;
and your love.

You made me better than I thought I could be.
And in my heart, you're still here with me.

BIBLIOGRAPHY & MUSIC REFERENCES

Bible references are all taken from the New International Version (MIV Life Application Study Bible – Hodder & Stoughton) unless stated that it has come from the RSV (Revised Standard Bible, Common Bible with Apocrypha - Collins).

Gill Beard – **Now is the Time** (Gill Beard, 1989)

Noel Brook & Pamela D Blair - **I Wasn't Ready to Say Goodbye: Surviving, Coping, and healing after the Sudden Death of a Loved One** (Source Books, 2008, ISBN: 3-978-1-89140-027-8)

Fiona Castle – **His Light in Our Darkness: An Anthology of Praise** (Hodder & Stoughton, 1985: ISBN – 0-340-90833-5)

Catherine Marshall – **To Live Again** (Evergreen Farm 2019, 1957, ISBN: ISBN: 978168370181)

Joyce Rupp – **Praying Our Goodbyes** (Ave Maria Press, 1998, 2008)

Liz McNeill Taylor – **Living With Loss: A Book for the Widowed** (Robinson, London, 1983: ISBN – 1-84119-105-1)

Joanna Weaver – **Having a Mary Heart in a Martha World** (Waterbrook Press, 2000, 2010: ISBN – 978-1-57856-258-9)

Mercy Me Songs – **Even If**
(https://www.youtube.com/watch?v=B6fA35Ved-Y)
The Hurt and the Healer
(https://www.youtube.com/watch?v=3xzaivDbu9c)
Mercy Me have a Facebook page

Useful Support Groups
WAY (Widowed and Young) support group
www.widowedandyoung.org.uk or look them up on Facebook
Care for the Family – www.careforthefamily.org.uk

Printed in Great Britain
by Amazon